COUNTRY SCENES
ADDRESS BOOK

Stephen Whittle

LITTLE, BROWN AND COMPANY
BOSTON TORONTO LONDON

First edition

ISBN 0 – 316 – 88895 – 8
A CIP catalogue record for this book is available from the British Library

Designed by Root Associates

Published simultaneously in the United States of America by Little, Brown and Company (Inc.), in Great Britain by Little, Brown and Company (UK) Ltd and in Canada by Little, Brown and Company (Canada) Limited.

PRINTED IN ITALY

FOREWORD

The inspiration for my work is the British countryside in its many forms. My etchings aim to recapture the atmosphere of a bygone, tranquil age when the slower pace of life allowed us more time to appreciate the colours and moods of our natural surroundings. Here you will find the winding lane, framed by flowery hedgerows; a gate is open; a cottage door stands ajar beckoning you in; the flowers themselves seem to nod their heads towards the horizon.

The rural buildings are often drawn from life, whether they are of Devon thatch, Cumbrian slate or honeyed Costwold stone. Other elements – flowers, trees, an old farm waggon – are drawn and re-drawn from sketches and photographs until the composition best mirrors the inner picture I seek to depict.

The craft of etching has changed little since it was first developed over 400 years ago. I coat a copper plate with a thin layer of acid-resisting wax. I then trace my design on to it and draw it with a sharp needle, each line revealing the bright copper. The plate is then immersed in acid which eats away at the copper exposed by the needle.

The next process, 'aquatint', allows me to strengthen the design by adding a range of tones to the line work. After the plates are etched and cleaned, coloured inks are mixed and paper dampened ready for printing. The system of colour printing which I use allows many colours to be applied to each plate with dabbers. After careful wiping the plates are placed on the bed of the press. My oldest press was made around 1910 and, as it turns, its mangle-like action exerts such pressure that the paper takes the ink with absolute fidelity. For each impression the plates must be inked and wiped again, making no two exactly identical.

I hope that this address book, which reproduces 22 of my etchings in colour, gives you as much pleasure as I had in making the originals.

Stephen Whittle

Stephen Whittle, Skelmersdale, 1992

Thomas Hardy's Cottage

A

NAME

ADDRESS

TELEPHONE

NAME

ADDRESS

TELEPHONE

NAME

ADDRESS

TELEPHONE

NAME

ADDRESS

TELEPHONE

NAME

ADDRESS

TELEPHONE

NAME

ADDRESS

TELEPHONE

NAME

ADDRESS

TELEPHONE

NAME

ADDRESS

TELEPHONE

A

NAME

ADDRESS

TELEPHONE

NAME

ADDRESS

TELEPHONE

NAME

ADDRESS

TELEPHONE

NAME

ADDRESS

TELEPHONE

NAME

ADDRESS

TELEPHONE

NAME

ADDRESS

TELEPHONE

NAME

ADDRESS

TELEPHONE

NAME

ADDRESS

TELEPHONE

A

NAME

ADDRESS

TELEPHONE

NAME

ADDRESS

TELEPHONE

NAME

ADDRESS

TELEPHONE

NAME

ADDRESS

TELEPHONE

NAME

ADDRESS

TELEPHONE

NAME

ADDRESS

TELEPHONE

NAME

ADDRESS

TELEPHONE

NAME

ADDRESS

TELEPHONE

B

NAME
ADDRESS

TELEPHONE

NAME
ADDRESS

TELEPHONE

NAME
ADDRESS

TELEPHONE

NAME
ADDRESS

TELEPHONE

NAME
ADDRESS

TELEPHONE

NAME
ADDRESS

TELEPHONE

NAME
ADDRESS

TELEPHONE

NAME
ADDRESS

TELEPHONE

B

NAME

ADDRESS

TELEPHONE

NAME

ADDRESS

TELEPHONE

NAME

ADDRESS

TELEPHONE

NAME

ADDRESS

TELEPHONE

NAME

ADDRESS

TELEPHONE

NAME

ADDRESS

TELEPHONE

NAME

ADDRESS

TELEPHONE

NAME

ADDRESS

TELEPHONE

Harvest Poppies

C

NAME

ADDRESS

TELEPHONE

NAME

ADDRESS

TELEPHONE

NAME

ADDRESS

TELEPHONE

NAME

ADDRESS

TELEPHONE

NAME

ADDRESS

TELEPHONE

NAME

ADDRESS

TELEPHONE

NAME

ADDRESS

TELEPHONE

NAME

ADDRESS

TELEPHONE

C

NAME

ADDRESS

TELEPHONE

NAME

ADDRESS

TELEPHONE

NAME

ADDRESS

TELEPHONE

NAME

ADDRESS

TELEPHONE

NAME

ADDRESS

TELEPHONE

NAME

ADDRESS

TELEPHONE

NAME

ADDRESS

TELEPHONE

NAME

ADDRESS

TELEPHONE

C

NAME

ADDRESS

TELEPHONE

NAME

ADDRESS

TELEPHONE

NAME

ADDRESS

TELEPHONE

NAME

ADDRESS

TELEPHONE

NAME

ADDRESS

TELEPHONE

NAME

ADDRESS

TELEPHONE

NAME

ADDRESS

TELEPHONE

NAME

ADDRESS

TELEPHONE

D

NAME

ADDRESS

TELEPHONE

NAME

ADDRESS

TELEPHONE

NAME

ADDRESS

TELEPHONE

NAME

ADDRESS

TELEPHONE

NAME

ADDRESS

TELEPHONE

NAME

ADDRESS

TELEPHONE

NAME

ADDRESS

TELEPHONE

NAME

ADDRESS

TELEPHONE

Forgotten Village

D

NAME

ADDRESS

TELEPHONE

NAME

ADDRESS

TELEPHONE

NAME

ADDRESS

TELEPHONE

NAME

ADDRESS

TELEPHONE

NAME

ADDRESS

TELEPHONE

NAME

ADDRESS

TELEPHONE

NAME

ADDRESS

TELEPHONE

NAME

ADDRESS

TELEPHONE

D

NAME

ADDRESS

TELEPHONE

NAME

ADDRESS

TELEPHONE

NAME

ADDRESS

TELEPHONE

NAME

ADDRESS

TELEPHONE

NAME

ADDRESS

TELEPHONE

NAME

ADDRESS

TELEPHONE

NAME

ADDRESS

TELEPHONE

NAME

ADDRESS

TELEPHONE

E

Cornish Cottages

E

NAME

ADDRESS

TELEPHONE

NAME

ADDRESS

TELEPHONE

NAME

ADDRESS

TELEPHONE

NAME

ADDRESS

TELEPHONE

NAME

ADDRESS

TELEPHONE

NAME

ADDRESS

TELEPHONE

NAME

ADDRESS

TELEPHONE

NAME

ADDRESS

TELEPHONE

E

NAME

ADDRESS

TELEPHONE

NAME

ADDRESS

TELEPHONE

NAME

ADDRESS

TELEPHONE

NAME

ADDRESS

TELEPHONE

NAME

ADDRESS

TELEPHONE

NAME

ADDRESS

TELEPHONE

NAME

ADDRESS

TELEPHONE

NAME

ADDRESS

TELEPHONE

E

NAME

ADDRESS

TELEPHONE

NAME

ADDRESS

TELEPHONE

NAME

ADDRESS

TELEPHONE

NAME

ADDRESS

TELEPHONE

NAME

ADDRESS

TELEPHONE

NAME

ADDRESS

TELEPHONE

NAME

ADDRESS

TELEPHONE

NAME

ADDRESS

TELEPHONE

F

NAME

ADDRESS

TELEPHONE

NAME

ADDRESS

TELEPHONE

NAME

ADDRESS

TELEPHONE

NAME

ADDRESS

TELEPHONE

NAME

ADDRESS

TELEPHONE

NAME

ADDRESS

TELEPHONE

NAME

ADDRESS

TELEPHONE

NAME

ADDRESS

TELEPHONE

Meadow Flowers

F

NAME

ADDRESS

TELEPHONE

NAME

ADDRESS

TELEPHONE

NAME

ADDRESS

TELEPHONE

NAME

ADDRESS

TELEPHONE

NAME

ADDRESS

TELEPHONE

NAME

ADDRESS

TELEPHONE

NAME

ADDRESS

TELEPHONE

NAME

ADDRESS

TELEPHONE

F

NAME

ADDRESS

TELEPHONE

NAME

ADDRESS

TELEPHONE

NAME

ADDRESS

TELEPHONE

NAME

ADDRESS

TELEPHONE

NAME

ADDRESS

TELEPHONE

NAME

ADDRESS

TELEPHONE

NAME

ADDRESS

TELEPHONE

NAME

ADDRESS

TELEPHONE

Flatford Mill

G

NAME

ADDRESS

TELEPHONE

NAME

ADDRESS

TELEPHONE

NAME

ADDRESS

TELEPHONE

NAME

ADDRESS

TELEPHONE

NAME

ADDRESS

TELEPHONE

NAME

ADDRESS

TELEPHONE

NAME

ADDRESS

TELEPHONE

NAME

ADDRESS

TELEPHONE

G

NAME

ADDRESS

TELEPHONE

NAME

ADDRESS

TELEPHONE

NAME

ADDRESS

TELEPHONE

NAME

ADDRESS

TELEPHONE

NAME

ADDRESS

TELEPHONE

NAME

ADDRESS

TELEPHONE

NAME

ADDRESS

TELEPHONE

NAME

ADDRESS

TELEPHONE

G

NAME

ADDRESS

TELEPHONE

NAME

ADDRESS

TELEPHONE

NAME

ADDRESS

TELEPHONE

NAME

ADDRESS

TELEPHONE

NAME

ADDRESS

TELEPHONE

NAME

ADDRESS

TELEPHONE

NAME

ADDRESS

TELEPHONE

NAME

ADDRESS

TELEPHONE

H

NAME

ADDRESS

TELEPHONE

NAME

ADDRESS

TELEPHONE

NAME

ADDRESS

TELEPHONE

NAME

ADDRESS

TELEPHONE

NAME

ADDRESS

TELEPHONE

NAME

ADDRESS

TELEPHONE

NAME

ADDRESS

TELEPHONE

NAME

ADDRESS

TELEPHONE

Thatch and Roses

H

NAME

ADDRESS

TELEPHONE

NAME

ADDRESS

TELEPHONE

NAME

ADDRESS

TELEPHONE

NAME

ADDRESS

TELEPHONE

NAME

ADDRESS

TELEPHONE

NAME

ADDRESS

TELEPHONE

NAME

ADDRESS

TELEPHONE

NAME

ADDRESS

TELEPHONE

H

NAME

ADDRESS

TELEPHONE

NAME

ADDRESS

TELEPHONE

NAME

ADDRESS

TELEPHONE

NAME

ADDRESS

TELEPHONE

NAME

ADDRESS

TELEPHONE

NAME

ADDRESS

TELEPHONE

NAME

ADDRESS

TELEPHONE

NAME

ADDRESS

TELEPHONE

II

Sunlit Waters

I

NAME

ADDRESS

TELEPHONE

NAME

ADDRESS

TELEPHONE

NAME

ADDRESS

TELEPHONE

NAME

ADDRESS

TELEPHONE

NAME

ADDRESS

TELEPHONE

NAME

ADDRESS

TELEPHONE

NAME

ADDRESS

TELEPHONE

NAME

ADDRESS

TELEPHONE

J

NAME

ADDRESS

TELEPHONE

NAME

ADDRESS

TELEPHONE

NAME

ADDRESS

TELEPHONE

NAME

ADDRESS

TELEPHONE

NAME

ADDRESS

TELEPHONE

NAME

ADDRESS

TELEPHONE

NAME

ADDRESS

TELEPHONE

NAME

ADDRESS

TELEPHONE

J

NAME

ADDRESS

TELEPHONE

NAME

ADDRESS

TELEPHONE

NAME

ADDRESS

TELEPHONE

NAME

ADDRESS

TELEPHONE

NAME

ADDRESS

TELEPHONE

NAME

ADDRESS

TELEPHONE

NAME

ADDRESS

TELEPHONE

NAME

ADDRESS

TELEPHONE

K

NAME

ADDRESS

TELEPHONE

NAME

ADDRESS

TELEPHONE

NAME

ADDRESS

TELEPHONE

NAME

ADDRESS

TELEPHONE

NAME

ADDRESS

TELEPHONE

NAME

ADDRESS

TELEPHONE

NAME

ADDRESS

TELEPHONE

NAME

ADDRESS

TELEPHONE

Dove Cottage

K

NAME

ADDRESS

TELEPHONE

NAME

ADDRESS

TELEPHONE

NAME

ADDRESS

TELEPHONE

NAME

ADDRESS

TELEPHONE

NAME

ADDRESS

TELEPHONE

NAME

ADDRESS

TELEPHONE

NAME

ADDRESS

TELEPHONE

NAME

ADDRESS

TELEPHONE

K

NAME

ADDRESS

TELEPHONE

NAME

ADDRESS

TELEPHONE

NAME

ADDRESS

TELEPHONE

NAME

ADDRESS

TELEPHONE

NAME

ADDRESS

TELEPHONE

NAME

ADDRESS

TELEPHONE

NAME

ADDRESS

TELEPHONE

NAME

ADDRESS

TELEPHONE

L

Bridlepath

L

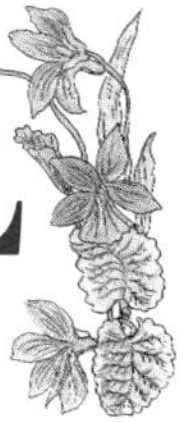

NAME

ADDRESS

TELEPHONE

NAME

ADDRESS

TELEPHONE

NAME

ADDRESS

TELEPHONE

NAME

ADDRESS

TELEPHONE

NAME

ADDRESS

TELEPHONE

NAME

ADDRESS

TELEPHONE

NAME

ADDRESS

TELEPHONE

NAME

ADDRESS

TELEPHONE

L

NAME

ADDRESS

TELEPHONE

NAME

ADDRESS

TELEPHONE

NAME

ADDRESS

TELEPHONE

NAME

ADDRESS

TELEPHONE

NAME

ADDRESS

TELEPHONE

NAME

ADDRESS

TELEPHONE

NAME

ADDRESS

TELEPHONE

NAME

ADDRESS

TELEPHONE

L

NAME

ADDRESS

TELEPHONE

NAME

ADDRESS

TELEPHONE

NAME

ADDRESS

TELEPHONE

NAME

ADDRESS

TELEPHONE

NAME

ADDRESS

TELEPHONE

NAME

ADDRESS

TELEPHONE

NAME

ADDRESS

TELEPHONE

NAME

ADDRESS

TELEPHONE

M

NAME

ADDRESS

TELEPHONE

NAME

ADDRESS

TELEPHONE

NAME

ADDRESS

TELEPHONE

NAME

ADDRESS

TELEPHONE

NAME

ADDRESS

TELEPHONE

NAME

ADDRESS

TELEPHONE

NAME

ADDRESS

TELEPHONE

NAME

ADDRESS

TELEPHONE

A Quiet Corner

M

NAME

ADDRESS

TELEPHONE

NAME

ADDRESS

TELEPHONE

NAME

ADDRESS

TELEPHONE

NAME

ADDRESS

TELEPHONE

NAME

ADDRESS

TELEPHONE

NAME

ADDRESS

TELEPHONE

NAME

ADDRESS

TELEPHONE

NAME

ADDRESS

TELEPHONE

M

NAME

ADDRESS

TELEPHONE

NAME

ADDRESS

TELEPHONE

NAME

ADDRESS

TELEPHONE

NAME

ADDRESS

TELEPHONE

NAME

ADDRESS

TELEPHONE

NAME

ADDRESS

TELEPHONE

NAME

ADDRESS

TELEPHONE

NAME

ADDRESS

TELEPHONE

Lakeland Flowers

N

NAME

ADDRESS

TELEPHONE

NAME

ADDRESS

TELEPHONE

NAME

ADDRESS

TELEPHONE

NAME

ADDRESS

TELEPHONE

NAME

ADDRESS

TELEPHONE

NAME

ADDRESS

TELEPHONE

NAME

ADDRESS

TELEPHONE

NAME

ADDRESS

TELEPHONE

N

NAME

ADDRESS

TELEPHONE

NAME

ADDRESS

TELEPHONE

NAME

ADDRESS

TELEPHONE

NAME

ADDRESS

TELEPHONE

NAME

ADDRESS

TELEPHONE

NAME

ADDRESS

TELEPHONE

NAME

ADDRESS

TELEPHONE

NAME

ADDRESS

TELEPHONE

N

NAME

ADDRESS

TELEPHONE

NAME

ADDRESS

TELEPHONE

NAME

ADDRESS

TELEPHONE

NAME

ADDRESS

TELEPHONE

NAME

ADDRESS

TELEPHONE

NAME

ADDRESS

TELEPHONE

NAME

ADDRESS

TELEPHONE

NAME

ADDRESS

TELEPHONE

O

NAME

ADDRESS

TELEPHONE

NAME

ADDRESS

TELEPHONE

NAME

ADDRESS

TELEPHONE

NAME

ADDRESS

TELEPHONE

NAME

ADDRESS

TELEPHONE

NAME

ADDRESS

TELEPHONE

NAME

ADDRESS

TELEPHONE

NAME

ADDRESS

TELEPHONE

Clematis at Dittisham

O

NAME

ADDRESS

TELEPHONE

NAME

ADDRESS

TELEPHONE

NAME

ADDRESS

TELEPHONE

NAME

ADDRESS

TELEPHONE

NAME

ADDRESS

TELEPHONE

NAME

ADDRESS

TELEPHONE

NAME

ADDRESS

TELEPHONE

NAME

ADDRESS

TELEPHONE

O

NAME

ADDRESS

TELEPHONE

NAME

ADDRESS

TELEPHONE

NAME

ADDRESS

TELEPHONE

NAME

ADDRESS

TELEPHONE

NAME

ADDRESS

TELEPHONE

NAME

ADDRESS

TELEPHONE

NAME

ADDRESS

TELEPHONE

NAME

ADDRESS

TELEPHONE

Spring Morning

P

NAME

ADDRESS

TELEPHONE

NAME

ADDRESS

TELEPHONE

NAME

ADDRESS

TELEPHONE

NAME

ADDRESS

TELEPHONE

NAME

ADDRESS

TELEPHONE

NAME

ADDRESS

TELEPHONE

NAME

ADDRESS

TELEPHONE

NAME

ADDRESS

TELEPHONE

P

NAME

ADDRESS

TELEPHONE

NAME

ADDRESS

TELEPHONE

NAME

ADDRESS

TELEPHONE

NAME

ADDRESS

TELEPHONE

NAME

ADDRESS

TELEPHONE

NAME

ADDRESS

TELEPHONE

NAME

ADDRESS

TELEPHONE

NAME

ADDRESS

TELEPHONE

P

NAME
ADDRESS

TELEPHONE

NAME
ADDRESS

TELEPHONE

NAME
ADDRESS

TELEPHONE

NAME
ADDRESS

TELEPHONE

NAME
ADDRESS

TELEPHONE

NAME
ADDRESS

TELEPHONE

NAME
ADDRESS

TELEPHONE

NAME
ADDRESS

TELEPHONE

Q

NAME

ADDRESS

TELEPHONE

NAME

ADDRESS

TELEPHONE

NAME

ADDRESS

TELEPHONE

NAME

ADDRESS

TELEPHONE

NAME

ADDRESS

TELEPHONE

NAME

ADDRESS

TELEPHONE

NAME

ADDRESS

TELEPHONE

NAME

ADDRESS

TELEPHONE

Harvest Valley

R

NAME

ADDRESS

TELEPHONE

NAME

ADDRESS

TELEPHONE

NAME

ADDRESS

TELEPHONE

NAME

ADDRESS

TELEPHONE

NAME

ADDRESS

TELEPHONE

NAME

ADDRESS

TELEPHONE

NAME

ADDRESS

TELEPHONE

NAME

ADDRESS

TELEPHONE

NAME

ADDRESS

TELEPHONE

NAME

ADDRESS

TELEPHONE

NAME

ADDRESS

TELEPHONE

NAME

ADDRESS

TELEPHONE

NAME

ADDRESS

TELEPHONE

NAME

ADDRESS

TELEPHONE

NAME

ADDRESS

TELEPHONE

NAME

ADDRESS

TELEPHONE

Sunlit Forest

S

NAME

ADDRESS

TELEPHONE

NAME

ADDRESS

TELEPHONE

NAME

ADDRESS

TELEPHONE

NAME

ADDRESS

TELEPHONE

NAME

ADDRESS

TELEPHONE

NAME

ADDRESS

TELEPHONE

NAME

ADDRESS

TELEPHONE

NAME

ADDRESS

TELEPHONE

S

NAME

ADDRESS

TELEPHONE

NAME

ADDRESS

TELEPHONE

NAME

ADDRESS

TELEPHONE

NAME

ADDRESS

TELEPHONE

NAME

ADDRESS

TELEPHONE

NAME

ADDRESS

TELEPHONE

NAME

ADDRESS

TELEPHONE

NAME

ADDRESS

TELEPHONE

S

NAME

ADDRESS

TELEPHONE

NAME

ADDRESS

TELEPHONE

NAME

ADDRESS

TELEPHONE

NAME

ADDRESS

TELEPHONE

NAME

ADDRESS

TELEPHONE

NAME

ADDRESS

TELEPHONE

NAME

ADDRESS

TELEPHONE

NAME

ADDRESS

TELEPHONE

T

NAME

ADDRESS

TELEPHONE

NAME

ADDRESS

TELEPHONE

NAME

ADDRESS

TELEPHONE

NAME

ADDRESS

TELEPHONE

NAME

ADDRESS

TELEPHONE

NAME

ADDRESS

TELEPHONE

NAME

ADDRESS

TELEPHONE

NAME

ADDRESS

TELEPHONE

T

Spring Cottage

T

NAME

ADDRESS

TELEPHONE

NAME

ADDRESS

TELEPHONE

NAME

ADDRESS

TELEPHONE

NAME

ADDRESS

TELEPHONE

NAME

ADDRESS

TELEPHONE

NAME

ADDRESS

TELEPHONE

NAME

ADDRESS

TELEPHONE

NAME

ADDRESS

TELEPHONE

T

NAME

ADDRESS

TELEPHONE

NAME

ADDRESS

TELEPHONE

NAME

ADDRESS

TELEPHONE

NAME

ADDRESS

TELEPHONE

NAME

ADDRESS

TELEPHONE

NAME

ADDRESS

TELEPHONE

NAME

ADDRESS

TELEPHONE

NAME

ADDRESS

TELEPHONE

Summer Lane

U

NAME

ADDRESS

TELEPHONE

NAME

ADDRESS

TELEPHONE

NAME

ADDRESS

TELEPHONE

NAME

ADDRESS

TELEPHONE

NAME

ADDRESS

TELEPHONE

NAME

ADDRESS

TELEPHONE

NAME

ADDRESS

TELEPHONE

NAME

ADDRESS

TELEPHONE

V

NAME

ADDRESS

TELEPHONE

NAME

ADDRESS

TELEPHONE

NAME

ADDRESS

TELEPHONE

NAME

ADDRESS

TELEPHONE

NAME

ADDRESS

TELEPHONE

NAME

ADDRESS

TELEPHONE

NAME

ADDRESS

TELEPHONE

NAME

ADDRESS

TELEPHONE

V

NAME

ADDRESS

TELEPHONE

NAME

ADDRESS

TELEPHONE

NAME

ADDRESS

TELEPHONE

NAME

ADDRESS

TELEPHONE

NAME

ADDRESS

TELEPHONE

NAME

ADDRESS

TELEPHONE

NAME

ADDRESS

TELEPHONE

NAME

ADDRESS

TELEPHONE

W

NAME

ADDRESS

TELEPHONE

NAME

ADDRESS

TELEPHONE

NAME

ADDRESS

TELEPHONE

NAME

ADDRESS

TELEPHONE

NAME

ADDRESS

TELEPHONE

NAME

ADDRESS

TELEPHONE

NAME

ADDRESS

TELEPHONE

NAME

ADDRESS

TELEPHONE

Woodbury Village

W

NAME

ADDRESS

TELEPHONE

NAME

ADDRESS

TELEPHONE

NAME

ADDRESS

TELEPHONE

NAME

ADDRESS

TELEPHONE

NAME

ADDRESS

TELEPHONE

NAME

ADDRESS

TELEPHONE

NAME

ADDRESS

TELEPHONE

NAME

ADDRESS

TELEPHONE

W

NAME

ADDRESS

TELEPHONE

NAME

ADDRESS

TELEPHONE

NAME

ADDRESS

TELEPHONE

NAME

ADDRESS

TELEPHONE

NAME

ADDRESS

TELEPHONE

NAME

ADDRESS

TELEPHONE

NAME

ADDRESS

TELEPHONE

NAME

ADDRESS

TELEPHONE

X

Woodland Walk

X

NAME

ADDRESS

TELEPHONE

NAME

ADDRESS

TELEPHONE

NAME

ADDRESS

TELEPHONE

NAME

ADDRESS

TELEPHONE

NAME

ADDRESS

TELEPHONE

NAME

ADDRESS

TELEPHONE

NAME

ADDRESS

TELEPHONE

NAME

ADDRESS

TELEPHONE

Y

NAME

ADDRESS

TELEPHONE

NAME

ADDRESS

TELEPHONE

NAME

ADDRESS

TELEPHONE

NAME

ADDRESS

TELEPHONE

NAME

ADDRESS

TELEPHONE

NAME

ADDRESS

TELEPHONE

NAME

ADDRESS

TELEPHONE

NAME

ADDRESS

TELEPHONE

Y

NAME

ADDRESS

TELEPHONE

NAME

ADDRESS

TELEPHONE

NAME

ADDRESS

TELEPHONE

NAME

ADDRESS

TELEPHONE

NAME

ADDRESS

TELEPHONE

NAME

ADDRESS

TELEPHONE

NAME

ADDRESS

TELEPHONE

NAME

ADDRESS

TELEPHONE

Z

NAME

ADDRESS

TELEPHONE

NAME

ADDRESS

TELEPHONE

NAME

ADDRESS

TELEPHONE

NAME

ADDRESS

TELEPHONE

NAME

ADDRESS

TELEPHONE

NAME

ADDRESS

TELEPHONE

NAME

ADDRESS

TELEPHONE

NAME

ADDRESS

TELEPHONE